THE UNITED STATE

monetary

history

By
Leo Barnes

Copyright © by Leo Barnes 2023). All rights reserved. This document must first have permission from the publisher before being copied or otherwise replicated. As a result, the information contained inside cannot be transferred electronically or stored in a database. The document cannot be copied, scanned, faxed, or retained in whole or in part without the publisher's permission.

TABLE OF CONTENTS

*The United States' First Bank

*United States Second Bank

*time of free banking

*United States national banks

*Historical perspectives on financial policy

*Three fundamental tenets of sound monetary policy

*Rules to Determine Monetary Policy

*Tackling the issue of bank panics

*Fluctuations

*Federal money

*Bank supervision

responsibility for oversight and regulation

*system for domestic payments

*Board of Governors of the Federal Reserve

*Associated banks

*Bank-to-bank lending

*The economy and inflation

Introduction

The colonial era, which is when the history of money in the United States starts, saw the use of a variety of currencies, including **English pounds**, **Spanish dollars**, and **wampum**. In **1792**, the **US government** declared the **US dollar** to be the country's legal tender. Under the gold standard, the US dollar's value was fixed at a set amount of gold in the late **19th century. During the Great Depression of the 1930s**, this was abandoned, and the US dollar subsequently changed into a fiat currency that was not backed by any specific item. The US dollar continues to play a large role in the country's monetary system and is still a major reserve currency on a global level. The creation of a national banking system was fiercely opposed by some of the Founding Fathers, and for many of them, the British attempt to subject the colonies to the Bank of England's monetary power was the "last straw" of oppression that sparked the American Revolutionary War. Others enthusiastically supported a national bank. Since 1782, when **Robert Morris** was acting as the Superintendent of Finance, **Thomas Goddard** has referred to **Robert Morris** as "the father of the system of credit and paper circulation in the United States." Following in the footsteps of the **Bank of England**, whose authority to issue bills of credit had been granted by the ***ratification of the Articles of Confederation in early 1781, Congress*** eventually passed an ordinance to incorporate a privately subscribed national bank. It was unable to fulfill its intended role as a national bank because of complaints of "alarming foreign influence and fictitious credit, toward foreigners, and unfair policies against less corrupt state banks issuing their own notes," and in ***1785 Pennsylvania's legislature*** repealed its charter to operate within the Commonwealth.

The United States' First Bank

To ensure the continuation of Morris's Bank project in 1791,

Alexander Hamilton, Secretary of the Treasury and former Morris aide, reached a compromise with Southern legislators. In return for the South's support for a national bank, Hamilton agreed to ensure enough support to move the national or federal capital from its temporary Northern location, New York, to a "Southern" location on the Potomac. As a result, Congress authorized the First Bank of the

United States (*1791–1811*) within the year, and *George Washington* signed it shortly after. *The First Bank of the United States*, which was based on the *Bank of England,* was very different from modern central banks in many aspects. For instance, it had foreign investors who received a portion of the company's income. Additionally, it wasn't solely accountable for the availability of currency in the nation. It was only in charge of 20% of the currency supply; the remainder was handled by state banks. A number of the founding fathers fiercely opposed the Bank. Thomas Jefferson perceived it as a catalyst for fraud, financial manipulation, and speculative activity. Its twenty-year charter expired in 1811, and Congress did not extend it. Without the federally authorized bank, the government printed a large number of Treasury Notes over the following years to create credit as it battled to pay for the War of 1812; most banks also quickly stopped accepting cash payments.

United States Second Bank

The federal government chartered its successor, the Second Bank of the United States, after five years

(1816–1836). *James Madison* ratified the constitution to halt the spiraling inflation that had afflicted the nation for the previous five years. It had locations all around the country and was essentially a replica of the First Bank. *President Andrew Jackson*, who took office in *1829*, criticized the bank as a source of corruption. As Democrats in the states opposed banks and Whigs supported

them, his destruction of the bank became a contentious political issue in the *1830s* and helped to create the Second Party System. Although he was unable to abolish the bank, he refused to extend its charter. *Jackson* made an effort to combat this by issuing an executive order mandating that all payments for federal land be made in gold or silver, by his understanding of the United

States Constitution, which only grants Congress the authority to "coin" money and not issues bills of credit. **Then came the Panic of 1837.** The Bank then categorically declined a demand to look through its archives, and its ***CEO, Nicholas Biddle***, pondered that it would be ironic if he were to end up in jail "by the votes of members of Congress because I would not hand up to their adversaries their confidential letters." Despite the dishonesty in Congress, Biddle was eventually taken into custody and accused of fraud. In 1836, the Bank's charter came to an end.

time of free banking

All banks during this time were state-chartered. The state's tightly regulated banks own reserve requirements, interest rates for loans and deposits, the minimum capital ratio, and other factors. They may issue bank notes against specie (gold and silver coins), but they might also issue notes against other assets. Parallel to the Banks of America, these institutions have been around since 1781. A bank that met the conditions might be automatically chartered without additional state legislative approval. Because governmental control was reduced in states that enacted it, it became simpler to establish unstable banks. Bank bills frequently had a lower real worth than their face value, and the magnitude of the discount was typically determined by the financial stability of the issuing bank. When the free banking era began *(1837)*, there were **24 chartered banks in the United States**; by **1863**, a privately issued note had been created, and there were **_712 institutions_**. With an average tenure of five years, banks during the free banking era were very short-lived in comparison to commercial banks today. About one-third of the banks went out of business due to their inability to redeem their notes, and about half of the banks collapsed. During the free banking era, a few neighborhood banks assumed control of a central bank's operations. Deposit insurance for member banks was offered in *New York* through **the *New York Safety Fund*. In Boston**, the *Suffolk Bank* served as both a private bank note issuer and a guaranteeing institution that banknotes would trade at close to par value.

United States national banks

to establish a network of national banks. In comparison

to state banks, they were expected to have better criteria for reserves and conduct of operations. State monopoly banks had the lowest long-term survival rates, according to recent research. To oversee these banks, the Comptroller of the Currency position was established. to establish a standard national currency. All national banks had to accept one another's currencies at face value to accomplish this. This removed the possibility of loss in the event of bank failure. The Comptroller of the Currency printed the notes to maintain consistency in quality and guard against forgery. National banks were compelled to hold Treasury securities to protect their notes to finance the war, expanding the market and increasing liquidity. Gresham's Law states that the government put a 10%

tax on state bank bills, which forced the majority of banks to become national banks, and that soon the bad money from state banks pushed out the new, good money. **There were 1,500 national banks in existence by 1865.** Only *325* state banks faced off against *1,638* national banks in *1870*. Checking accounts were developed and widely used as a result of the levy in the 1880s and 1890s. 90%

of the money supply was in checking and savings accounts by the 1890s. State-run banking had returned. There were still two issues with the banking industry. The first was the need for treasuries to back up the currency. Banks were forced to recall loans, borrow from other banks, or use clearinghouses when the value of treasuries fluctuated. The system's ability to produce seasonal liquidity surges was the second issue. When cash was most needed, such as during planting season, a rural bank withdrew from deposit accounts at a larger bank. The bank once more had to locate a lender of last resort when the combined liquidity demands were too high. Bank runs resulting from these liquidity crises caused significant disruptions and depressions, the worst of which was the **Panic of 1907. National Bank Notes** were issued by **national banks as money.** In contrast to notes issued during the Free Banking era, which may have drastically varying values depending on which bank issued them, they were uniformly backed by US government debt and as a result, they typically traded at comparable values. However, according to the National Bank Act, national bank notes were not "lawful tender" and could not be used as bank reserves. Along with gold, the United States issued greenbacks to serve this purpose. Early in the Civil War, in 1861, Congress stopped the gold standard and started printing paper money The Specie Payment Resumption Act of 1875 called for the eventual replacement of the federally printed greenbacks with national bank notes. The greenbacks were still in use and their eradication of them was deferred in 1878. Throughout the period, gold was still used to settle the federal debt. All forms of currency may be exchanged for gold once the United States went back to the gold standard in 1879.

Historical perspectives on financial policy

Inflation and deflation have both occurred sometimes in the United States throughout the past century, with periods of rising overall prices for goods and services being known as inflation and rare periods of dropping overall prices being known as deflation. After World

War I and for the first few years of the Great Depression, consumer prices dropped dramatically. Inflation briefly exceeded 10% annually in the 1970s and early 1980s as consumer prices increased at an ever-increasing rate. Contrarily, consumer price inflation has largely been low and consistent since the mid-1980s.

American families frequently perceive substantial and abrupt fluctuations in consumer prices both increases and decrease as a serious economic issue. Some of these price fluctuations were partially a sign of more serious economic problems, such as the Great Depression's skyrocketing unemployment. Large price changes might also be expensive on their own. Transfers of purchasing power, such as those between savers and borrowers, can occur when prices shift unexpectedly; these transfers are arbitrary and may appear unfair. Additionally, the uncertainty around the evolution of the price level and the unpredictability of inflation makes it harder to decide how much money to save and invest. High rates of inflation and deflation also necessitate more frequent contract revisions, menu and catalog revisions, and adjustments to tax rates and deductions. Price stability, or low and stable inflation, as it is now understood, raises American citizens' levels of living for all of these and other reasons. Although a variety of factors, such as fluctuations in the economy, the cost of commodities globally, the value of the dollar, taxes, and other factors, can influence the level of prices at any given time, the central bank is ultimately responsible for determining the average rate of inflation over a long period. The interaction between the general demand for goods and services and the costs of producing those goods and services determines whether prices increase or decrease on average over time and how quickly. *Particularly when people start to anticipate growing inflation, a combination of consistently faster growth in demand for goods and services than in the capacity to create them can cause it to rise.* Deflation, on the other hand, can result from continuously low demand for *products and services*, particularly when consumers anticipate further price declines. *The overall growth in demand for goods and services relative to growth in the economy's productive capacity is influenced by monetary policy's effects* on financial conditions and inflation expectations, and as a result, it has a significant impact on how inflation and the economy as a whole are managed. Furthermore, monetary policy works best when the public has faith that the central bank will take action to maintain steady and low inflation. Different nominal anchors have historically been used or proposed in the US and other nations to ensure that central banks controlled financial conditions in a way consistent with ensuring low and stable inflation over time. A nominal anchor is a variable that is believed to have a consistent relationship over time to the price level or the rate of inflation, such as the price of a certain good, an exchange rate, or the money supply. *The adoption of a nominal anchor is meant to assist firms and individuals in developing expectations about how monetary policy will be implemented and future inflation.* Stable inflation expectations can then assist in stabilizing actual inflation. The gold standard, which functioned as the notional anchor for most of the world, including the United States, at the time the Federal Reserve was established in 1913, is one notable example. Under the gold standard, the central bank agrees to exchange, upon request, a unit of the country's money (**such as a dollar**) for a specific amount of gold. As a result, the amount of money in the economy changes together with the amount of gold stored in the vaults of the central bank. The price level can be anticipated to be roughly steady if gold output keeps pace with economic expansion and the convertibility of gold into other currencies is faithfully upheld. The upkeep of a fixed currency rate is one example that is related. A unit of domestic currency may be purchased or sold for a specific amount of foreign money under a fixed exchange rate regime (as opposed to a fixed amount of gold, as in the case of the gold standard. A nation with a fixed exchange rate often experiences inflation over time that is comparable to that of the foreign economy with which it is fixed. Due to this, nations with a history of high or volatile inflation have frequently thought about tying their monetary policy to that of a sizable nation, like the United States or Germany, that has had relative success establishing low and stable inflation. Targeting the money supply is an additional illustration of a nominal anchor. In this strategy, the central bank gradually increases the money supply at a predetermined, often set, rate. The central bank hopes to restrict variations in the inflation rate by limiting the growth of the money supply. Many central banks, including the Fed, adopted such targets into their policy frameworks to assist lower the inflation rate from the high levels experienced in the 1970s. The United States experience with these nominal anchors in practice has brought to light several practical difficulties. In the case of the gold standard, maintaining the ability to convert money into gold on demand was not always consistent with maintaining price stability. When gold output lagged behind economic growth, the United States frequently experienced deflation; conversely, when gold production outpaced economic expansion, inflation was more common.

Early in the 20th century, for instance, the introduction of the cyanide extraction method, which enhanced the quantity of gold recovered from low-grade ore, *and significant gold discoveries in important countries and elsewhere increased* the **supply of gold** and helped ***raise the U.S. price level***, Discoveries of gold anywhere in the world could increase U.S. inflation since gold could be transported easily across nations. Another issue is that the policies necessary to uphold the gold standard can occasionally harm employment and economic activity, especially during times of economic unrest. Due in part to the fact that the amount of gold stored in many central banks' vaults was frequently less than the total amount of currency in circulation, these institutions kept close tabs on their gold holdings. *This condition encouraged people to exchange their money for gold in advance whenever they were concerned that the central bank could run out of gold.* Central banks occasionally tried to attract gold by boosting interest rates to prevent runs on their gold holdings and maintain the gold standard. Greater interest rates encouraged both domestic and foreign investors to convert their overseas holdings into gold, transport that gold to the nation that had hiked interest rates, and then exchange that gold for local currency at the central bank to invest in domestic assets with higher yields. However, higher interest rates would slow the economy and raise the unemployment rate. Maintaining the gold standard with such measures in the 1930s is likely to have made the Great Depression worse in several nations, including the

United States. As a result, the gold standard was eventually abandoned, and efforts were made to develop more suitable monetary systems in the ***post-World War II era.***

Fixed exchange rate systems frequently come with difficulties similar to those of the gold standard. Under fixed exchange rates, the requirement to keep the exchange rate at the desired level takes precedence over a central bank's ability to employ monetary policy to respond to domestic economic circumstances. People must have faith in the central bank's capacity to convert local currency into foreign currency on demand by maintaining sufficient levels of foreign currency reserves and willingness to protect the exchange rate against speculative attacks for fixed exchange rate regimes to be long-lasting (by raising interest rates even if it would cause the economy to fall into recession. If not, people can try to prevent a crisis in the foreign exchange market by proactively converting their local currency holdings into foreign currency assets to protect their wealth. Since investors believed that the monetary policy required to achieve domestic policy objectives was incompatible with the monetary policy pursued by the anchor-currency country and believed that the domestic central bank would place a higher priority on achieving domestic goals than on maintaining the exchange rate, many fixed exchange rate regimes have ended in crisis. Targeting the expansion of the money supply presented a different kind of difficulty. In the *1970s* and *1980s*, several central banks, including the Fed, tried to control inflation by establishing a money supply target, but they discovered that there was a shaky correlation between inflation, economic activity, and money growth indicators.

The financial industry underwent part of considerable innovation and transformation throughout this time. The pace of money growth that is consistent with price stability became extremely unclear in part as a result.

Three fundamental tenets of sound monetary policy

Several fundamental guidelines for the conduct of monetary policy have been developed over the past few decades by policymakers and academic economists; these guidelines are based on historical experience with a variety of monetary policy frameworks. The well-organized and systematic nature of monetary policy is one of the guiding principles. The public should be informed of and understand the explicit goals of monetary policy. The goals of American monetary policy are to achieve maximum employment and price stability, and Congress has instructed the Federal Reserve to do so. *In Monetary Policy?* Fed policymakers provide a summary of their understanding of that statutory mandate. To be systematic, policymakers should react to changes in economic conditions and the economic outlook consistently and predictably. They should also clearly communicate their policy strategy and actions to the public, and they should stick to previous policy announcements and communications unless new information requires them to revise earlier plans. By avoiding unexpected policy changes, this approach encourages economic stability by assisting individuals and businesses in making decisions about their finances and plans. The second tenet is that when both inflation and economic activity are below the levels necessary for full resource consumption, the central bank should use monetary and fiscal policy stimulus. In contrast, when the economy is overheated and inflation exceeds its target, the central bank should adopt a restrictive monetary policy. The central bank should sometimes proactively abide by this rule. For instance, economic developments like a significant and unanticipated change in financial conditions may not immediately affect inflation and employment but will do so in the future, necessitating a fast and proactive policy reaction. It can be challenging to explain how monetary policy would react to unpredictable future events, but the fundamental idea is the same: Policymakers should work to explain how these events might influence the trajectory of inflation and employment in the future and adjust monetary policy as necessary. Thirdly, the central bank should adjust the policy interest rate more than one-for-one higher over time in response to persistently rising inflation and more than one-for-one lower over time in reaction to persistently falling inflation. The central bank should increase the policy rate by more than one percentage point, for instance, if the inflation rate increases from 1 percent to 2 percent without being the result of temporary circumstances. The real policy rate, which is the level of the policy rate adjusted for inflation, increases with rising inflation and decreases with falling inflation as a result of this adjustment to the policy rate. Inflation-adjusted real interest rates that affect how expensive it is for consumers and businesses to borrow money to support consumption or investment spending are fed through by other real interest rates as the real policy rate rises.

Raising real interest rates tends to limit economic growth, as businesses raise prices more slowly when their sales are growing more slowly. Inflation is then kept under control. The central bank's response to ongoing inflation declines follows some homogeneous rationale.

Rules to Determine Monetary Policy

According to some academic studies on policy rules, connecting monetary policy to a straightforward and constant policy rule can streamline the central bank's communications with the public and make monetary policy predictable and reasonably simple to understand. According to this argument, adhering to a straightforward policy rule could potentially increase the effectiveness of monetary policy by guiding households' and businesses' expectations of future economic and financial conditions expectations that affect consumer spending and business investment for a discussion of the significance of expectations in the transmission of monetary policy to the broader economy in the real world, the structure of the economy changes over time, and those, For example, the value of the neutral federal funds rate in economies all over the world appears to have decreased in the wake of the Global Financial Crisis when expressed as rLT, the longer run adjusted for inflation. Estimates for the US indicate that rLT has decreased from a little bit over 2% before the Global Financial Crisis to about 1% or less in recent years.

The median projected longer-run federal funds rate adjusted for inflation decreased from 2.25 percent in January 2012 to 0.75 percent in September 2017 in the forecasts that each member of the Board of Governors and each Federal Reserve Bank president submits each quarter and that are published in the *Summary of Economic Projections*. According to some theories, the lower level of rLT is caused by a variety of variables, such as a slower rate of productivity growth, demographic changes brought on by population aging, worldwide patterns of saving and investing, and a shift in demand toward more "safe" assets. This means that neutral rates may continue to be low for some time as many of these factors look likely to last, changing the rule to account for the decline in the value of *rLT* would be necessary if monetary policy were governed by a straightforward rule. Inaction would lead to poor policy decisions. In such cases, it's possible that the regulation won't improve the public's comprehension of monetary policy or the clarity of the central bank's communications. *Frequent revisions to the policy norm could harm the central bank's reputation and undermine the legitimacy of its strategy.* The economic models that academic researchers typically employ also assume that any unexpected events that will affect the economy in the future will resemble unexpected events that occurred in the past, that is, that the types and range of shocks affecting the economy in the future will not be that different from the shocks that have already hit the economy, and that these assumptions will be true regardless of how simple the policy rule is. However, in reality, economic shocks can and do vary over time in terms of their nature and size. *It is not always the case that a straightforward policy rule that produces positive economic performance under one set of shocks will produce positive economic performance under another set of shocks.* Additionally, the academic research literature on policy rules frequently assumes that *individuals and organizations* will fully and instantly comprehend what the rule would instruct the central bank to do in all potential future economic scenarios as well as the effects of that decision on the economy. The advantages that the models claim for simple rules will not be fully realized if these presumptions are not true in the real world. Last but not least, economists often utilize models that assume that the economic downside and upside risks are "symmetric," or equal. In certain situations, the risks related to the economic outlook may be greatly skewed or asymmetric. Such disparities are not taken into consideration by simple policy principles. Asymmetric risk need not necessarily support a more gradual course; if risks were highly skewed toward sustained overheating and excessive inflation, the asymmetric risk could support higher rates than suggested by straightforward rules. Changing or amending the rule to account for the decline in the value of rLT would be necessary if monetary policy were governed by a straightforward rule. Inaction would lead to poor policy decisions. In such cases, it's possible that the regulation won't improve the public's comprehension of monetary policy or the clarity of the central bank's communications. In reality, changes to the policy norm may harm the central bank's reputation and the legitimacy of its policy, especially if they happen frequently. The economic models that academic researchers typically employ also assume that any unexpected events that will affect the economy in the future will resemble unexpected events that occurred in the past, the that the types and range of shocks affecting the economy in the future will not be that different from the shocks that have already hit the economy, and that these assumptions will be true regardless of how simple the policy rule is. A straightforward policy rule that produces positive economic performance under one set of shocks may not necessarily provide positive economic performance in a second set of shocks because, in reality, the type and size of the shocks that affect the economy can and do change over time. Additionally, the academic research literature on policy rules frequently assumes that individuals and organizations will fully and instantly comprehend what the rule would instruct the central bank to do in all potential future economic scenarios as well as the effects of that decision on the economy. The benefits of using simple rules, as claimed by the models, won't be completely realized if these presumptions are incorrect in the real world.

Last but not least, economists often utilize models that assume that the economic downside and upside risks are "symmetric," or equal. In certain situations, the risks related to the economic outlook may be greatly skewed or asymmetric. Such inequalities are not considered in simple policy rules. Asymmetric risk need not necessarily support a more gradual course; if risks were highly skewed toward sustainable significantly and excessive inflation. *the asymmetric risk could support higher rates than suggested by straightforward rules.* As previously mentioned, some *academic research on policy rules suggests that connecting monetary policy to a straightforward, unchanging policy rule may improve its efficacy by assisting in guiding households' and enterprises' expectations of future economic and financial situations.* To profit from managing expectations, the central bank does not necessarily need to bind the monetary policy to a clear-cut rule. Experience and academic research indicate that another way to achieve those benefits is a clear commitment to explicit goals, *along with policy transparency and clear communication* that enables the public to understand how the central bank's policy actions related to its goals; these essential elements of the policy framework are currently followed by the Fed and other significant central banks. This framework is examined in the Monetary Policy Strategies of Major Central Banks.

tackling the issue of bank panics

In the United States, banks are required to retain reserves, which are sums of money and deposits in other institutions, but only to an extent sufficient to cover their client deposit responsibilities. Banking with a fractional reserve is this technique. Banks typically invest the majority of the money they receive in deposits as a result. A bank run occurs when too many bank clients withdraw their savings at once, forcing the bank to seek assistance from another institution to stay open. Bank robberies can result in a wide range of social and economic issues. The Federal Reserve System was created to stop or lessen bank runs and may even function as a lender of last choice when one does happen. A check-clearing system was established inside the Federal Reserve System because, during periods of economic turbulence, some banks refused to clear checks from specific other banks. Congress wanted to end the severe financial crises that had periodically swept the country by establishing the Federal Reserve System, notably the type of financial panic that happened in 1907. Payments were interrupted nationwide during that incident as a result of numerous banks and clearinghouses refusing to cash checks drawn on specific other institutions; *this practice ultimately led to the demise of several otherwise solvent banks.* Congress granted the Federal Reserve System the ability to create a national check-clearing system to address these issues.

Therefore, the Mechanism was to provide both an effective and fair check-collection system in addition to elastic money, or a currency that would change in value in response to changes in the economy. *The Federal Reserve* acts as the institution's lender of last resort in the United States for those institutions that are unable to receive credit from other sources and whose failure would have a significant negative impact on the economy. During the Free Banking Era, the private sector "clearing houses" served this function; whether public or private, the availability of liquidity was meant to stop bank runs.

Fluctuations

The Reserve Banks offer banks liquidity through their credit operations and discount window to cover short-term needs brought on by erratic seasonal deposit patterns or unforeseen withdrawals. In certain cases, longer-term liquidity may also be given. The Fed charges banks a discount rate "formally the primary credit rate" for these loans. The Fed provides a cushion with these loans against unforeseen daily variations in reserve availability and demand. The banking system benefits from this as it relieves pressure on the reserve market and lessens the impact of unforeseen changes in interest rates. For instance, the Federal Reserve Board sanctioned an $85 billion loan on September 16, 2008, to prevent *the global insurance juggernaut American International Group from going bankrupt (AIG).* The Federal Reserve acts as both the government's bank and a bank for bankers in its capacity as the nation's central bank. It contributes to ensuring the effectiveness and safety of the payments system as the banker's bank. The Fed manages a wide range of financial transactions involving trillions of dollars as the bank or fiscal agent of the government. The U.S. Treasury maintains a checking account with the Federal Reserve, much like an individual could do, through which incoming federal tax deposits and outgoing government payments are managed. The Fed sells and redeems U.S. government assets, including Treasury bills, notes, and bonds, as part of its service arrangement. It also produces coin and paper money for the country. The U.S. The Treasury creates the country's currency through the Bureau of the Mint and the Bureau of Engraving and Printing, which in turn sells the paper money to the Federal

Reserve Banks at production cost and the coins at face value. The Federal Reserve Banks then disperse it in a variety of ways to other financial entities. *The Bureau of Engraving and Printing produced 57.95 billion notes in Fiscal Year 2020 at an average cost of 7.4 cents each.*

federal money

The reserve balances (also known as Federal Reserve Deposits) that private banks retain at their neighborhood Federal Reserve Bank are known as federal funds. The Federal Reserve System's eponymous reserves are these balances. To provide a means for private banks to lend money to one another, money is kept in a Federal Reserve Bank. As the source of the Federal Reserve System's name and the foundation for monetary policy, this market for funds has a significant impact on the organization. The amount of interest that private banks charge one another for lending out these funds is one way that monetary policy is implemented.

Federal Reserve Credit, which can be exchanged into Federal Reserve Notes, is kept in Federal Reserve Accounts. Bank reserves held by private banks are kept in federal reserve accounts.

Bank supervision

Private banks are regulated by the Federal Reserve. A compromise between the opposing ideologies of privatization and government regulation resulted in the creation of the system.

The system's organizational structure also reflects the harmony between commercial interests and the state. While the members of the board of governors are chosen by the President of the United States and confirmed by the Senate, private banks elect the board of directors at their local Federal Reserve Bank. The economy, monetary policy, banking supervision and regulation, consumer credit protection, financial markets, and other topics are regularly the subject of their testimony before congressional committees. The Board communicates often with the President's Council of Economic Advisers as well as other important economic leaders. The United States President and the Secretary of the Treasury both occasionally meet with the Chair, who also does so regularly. Additionally, the Chair is charged with official duties abroad.

responsibility for oversight and regulation

Each Federal Reserve Bank District's board of directors is also charged with regulatory and oversight duties. A district bank's board of directors will inform the board of governors if it believes a member bank is performing or acting in an unsatisfactory manner. *To determine whether bank credit is being used inadvertently* for the speculative holding or trading of securities, real estate, or commodities, or for any other purpose failure to comply with the preservation of sound credit standards, each Federal reserve bank shall keep itself informed of the general character and amount of the loans and investments of its member banks. And, in deciding whether to grant or refuse advances, rediscounts, or other credit accounts. *Any such unauthorized use of bank credit by a member bank must be reported by the chairman of the Federal Reserve Bank, together with his suggestion, to the Board of Governors of the Federal Reserve System.* Anytime a member bank improperly uses bank credit, in the opinion of the Board of Governors of the Federal Reserve System, the Board may, at its discretion, suspend the member bank from using the credit facilities of the Federal Reserve System. The suspension may be terminated at any time or renewed periodically.

system for domestic payments

The American payments system includes involvement from the Federal Reserve. Depository institutions and the federal government both get banking services from the twelve Federal Reserve Banks. For depository institutions, manage accounts and offer a range of payment services, including check collection, electronic fund transfers, and the distribution and receipt of cash and coin. The Reserve Banks function as fiscal agents for the federal government and local states, processing electronic payments, issuing, transferring, and redeeming U.S. government securities, as well as paying Treasury checks. Congress reiterated that the Federal Reserve should support a productive national payments system in the Depository

Institutions Deregulation and Monetary Control Act of 1980. The statute makes reserve requirements applicable to all depository institutions, not only member commercial banks and gives them equal access to Reserve Bank payment services. By offering financial services to depository institutions, the Federal Reserve contributes to the nation's retail and wholesale payment networks. Retail payments typically include the small-business and individual clients of a depository institution and are for relatively little sums of money. Distribution of money and coins, check collection, and electronic money transfers via the automated clearing house system are all included in the retail services provided by the Reserve Banks System for domestic payments

The American payments system includes involvement from the Federal Reserve. Depository institutions and the federal government both get banking services from the twelve Federal Reserve Banks. For depository institutions, manage accounts and offer a range of payment services, including check collection, electronic fund transfers, and the distribution and receipt of cash and coin.

The Reserve Banks function as fiscal agents for the federal government and local states' electronic payments, issuing, transferring, and redeeming U.S. government securities, as well as paying Treasury checks, Congress reiterated that the Federal Reserve should support a productive national payments system in the Depository Institutions Deregulation and Monetary Control Act of 1980.

The statute makes reserve requirements applicable to all depository institutions, not only member commercial banks and gives them equal access to Reserve Bank payment services. By offering financial services to depository institutions, the Federal Reserve contributes to the nation's retail and wholesale payment networks. Retail payments typically include the small-business and individual clients of a depository institution and are for relatively little sums of money. Distribution of money and coins, check collection, and electronic money transfers via the automated clearing house system are all included in the retail services provided by the Reserve Banks. A depository institution's major corporate clients, including other financial institutions, are frequently involved in wholesale payments, which typically include significant dollar sums.

The wholesale services provided by the Reserve Banks include the electronic transmission of cash via the Fedwire Funds Service and the transfer of securities issued by the United States government, its agencies, and specific other entities via the Fedwire Securities Services. The wholesale services provided by the Reserve Banks include the electronic transmission of cash via the Fedwire Funds

Service and the transfer of securities issued by the United States government, its agencies, and specific other entities via the Fedwire Securities Service.

Board of Governors of the Federal Reserve

A significant government organization with seven members, the board of governors performs business oversight by assessing national banks.: 12, 15 It is tasked with establishing national monetary policy and supervising the 12 District Reserve Banks. Additionally, it oversees and controls the whole U.S. banking sector. For staggered 14-year terms, governors are chosen by the president of the United States and confirmed by the Senate. Members serving a full term are ineligible to be renominated for another term, which starts every two years on February 1 of even-numbered years. Members of the Board are required to stay on after their terms are up until their chosen and qualified successors have been selected." According to the law, the president may dismiss a board member "for cause". The Speaker of the U.S. House of Representatives must receive an annual report from the board on its activities. The president selects the board of governors' chair and vice chair from among the currently serving governors. They each have a four-year term, and the president may nominate them again as many as they choose until the end of their board of governors terms.

Associated banks

A member bank is an exclusive organization that holds stock in the local Federal Reserve Bank. Every nationally incorporated bank owns shares in one of the Federal Reserve Banks. If state-licensed banks meet specific requirements, they may decide to join and own stock in their local Federal Reserve bank. A member bank's required stock holdings are equivalent to 3% of its total capital and surplus. But owning stock in a Federal Reserve bank is not the same as doing so in a publicly traded corporation. Because member banks cannot sell or exchange their shares, they do not influence the Federal Reserve

Bank. Member banks receive a dividend of 6% from their Regional Bank for assets of $10 billion or less, and whichever is less than 6% or the prevailing 10-year Treasury auction rate for assets of more than $10 billion. The United States Treasury Department receives the remaining earnings earned by the regional Federal Reserve Banks. The Federal Reserve Institutions generated a $100.2

billion profit in 2015, returned $97.7 billion to the U.S. Treasury, and paid out $2.5 billion in dividends to member banks. The regional Federal Reserve Bank is home to about 45% of American banks.

Bank-to-bank lending

By influencing the federal funds rate, which is the rate at which excess reserves are lent between banks, the Federal Reserve determines monetary policy. The interbank market determines the interest rates that banks charge one another for these loans, and the Federal Reserve affects these rates using the three "tools" of the monetary policy listed in the Tools section below. The FOMC places a lot of emphasis on the federal funds rate, a short-term interest rate that has an impact on the longer-term rates across the economy. By altering market conditions for balances that depository institutions keep at Federal Reserve Banks, the Federal Reserve carries out the monetary policy of the United States. The Federal Reserve exerts substantial control over the demand for and supply of Federal Reserve balances as well as the federal funds rate by carrying out open market operations, enforcing reserve requirements, allowing depository institutions to hold contractual clearing balances, and extending credit through its discount window facility. The Federal Reserve is in a position to promote economic and monetary conditions that are consistent with its monetary policy goals since it controls the federal funds rate. Targeting the federal funds rate is a key component of how the Federal

Reserve System carries out monetary policy. Federal funds, which are the reserves held by banks at the Fed, are lent overnight at this interest rate by banks to one another. The market sets this rate; the Federal does not demand it. Therefore, the Fed uses open market operations to increase or decrease the money supply to bring the effective federal funds rate into line with the targeted rate. The needed reserve ratio, commonly referred to as the fractional reserve requirement, was another tool the Federal Reserve System previously used to modify monetary policy. The required reserve ratio establishes the balance that a depository institution must maintain in the Federal Reserve Banks to transact business on the federal funds market previously mentioned. *The board of governors of the Federal Reserve System determines the necessary reserve ratio.* The Federal Reserve has produced a history of how the reserve requirements have varied throughout time. In response to the financial crisis of 2008, the Federal Reserve now pays interest on required and excess reserve amounts held by depository institutions. While keeping the federal funds rate near the target rate set by the FOMC, the central bank has more chances to address the state of the credit market thanks to the payment of interest on excess reserves. A bank is not needed to retain any reserves as of March 2020 because all banks have a 0% reserve ratio, essentially eliminating the reserve requirement.

The economy and inflation

The majority of conventional economists prefer a modest,

constant rate of inflation. *Chief economist Diane C. Swonk*, who also serves as an advisor to the Federal Reserve, the Congressional Budget Office, and the Council of Economic Advisers, noted in 2022 that "You must keep in mind that inflation is something similar to cancer from the standpoint of the Fed. If you don't take care of it right away, it can become painful later on and spread to other parts of your body, making it much more chronic. By allowing the labor market to respond more rapidly during a downturn and lowering the chance that a liquidity trap will prevent monetary policy from stabilizing the economy, low inflation as opposed to zero or negative inflation may lessen the severity of economic downturns. Typically, monetary authorities are tasked with maintaining a low and stable rate of inflation.

www.ingramcontent.com/pod-product-compliance
Lightning Source LLC
Chambersburg PA
CBHW070320220526
45465CB00013B/1390